100
Spiritual Drops

MiA, MAY GoD OPEN YOUR EYES To THE TRUTHS; WITHIN. GoD BLESS You BOTH.

James L. Gordon

5/24/18

100
Spiritual Drops

James L. Gordon

Published By:
Brentwood Christian Press
www.BrentwoodBooks.com
1-800-334-8861

Table of Contents

Introduction

To the reader: I take it by faith if you have this book in your hand, it's not a coincidence.

The writing of this book is by the inspiration of the Holy Spirit and my personal desire to share the many spiritual blessings that the Lord has rewarded me with, to help others.

After 24 years, and approximately three hundred and fifty cities later, along with an innumerable amount of hours of evangelizing and counseling of thousands of people, I still have my zeal to do the work of the Lord as a disciple, living by faith as described in Luke Chapter 10.

My first book title *Take It By Faith*, which was written in 1991, has the following statement in the introduction: "I began to write this book to help the many people who are lost and in a state of perpetual confusion, due to being blinded by their own pride." This has not changed much, except as man has progressed in his realm of intelligentsia, he has become more self-centered and self-serving.

For those of you who read this book who are not Christians, I understand your right of free choice as well as your own belief system which is an integral part of everyone's existence. My hope is that if you do read this book you will be as objective as you possibly can, without bias or religious prejudice.

1. Be <u>humble</u> in all areas of <u>your</u> life.

The proud and arrogant are always perturbed and agitated, while the humble and poor in spirit are peaceful and contented.

James 4:6 "<u>God</u> resists the proud but gives <u>grace</u> to the <u>humble</u>."

Your inspirational notes

_____

_____

_____

_____

_____

_____

_____

_____

_____

_____

2. Seek help with your problems.

   Asking for help is a true sign that you are just about to solve the problem or situation you're involved in.

   Psalms 3:2-3 "<u>Many</u> are they who say of me, "There is no <u>help</u> for him in <u>God</u>." But you, O Lord, are a <u>shield</u> for me. My <u>glory</u> and the one who <u>lifts</u> up my head."

Your inspirational notes

_____

_____

_____

_____

_____

_____

_____

_____

3. Don't help; help!!!

When asking for help, don't try and tell your help how to solve your situation. If you know how to solve it why are you seeking help, or is there a hidden agenda you're not revealing?

Hebrews 13:6 "So we may <u>boldly</u> say: "The Lord is my helper; I will not <u>fear</u>. What can man do to me?"

Your inspirational notes

_____

_____

_____

_____

_____

_____

_____

_____

4. Be kind to a stranger.

Be kind to a stranger, for in so doing you can truly pass on the love of God, and cause the person to ponder your act of kindness. The seed is planted and who knows how fruitful it will be.

> Isaiah 54:10 "For the mountains shall depart and the hills be removed, but my kindness shall not depart from you, nor shall my covenant of peace be removed, say the Lord, who has mercy on you."

Your inspirational notes

_____

_____

_____

_____

_____

_____

_____

5. Be charitable.

Truly you have been blessed, so share it with others to keep the channel of flow open and fresh. Like a fresh running stream is clean and healthy; so is one stagnant that is stopped and full of back wash."

Hebrews 7:7 "It is beyond dispute that the <u>inferior</u> is blessed by the <u>superior</u>."

Your inspirational notes

_____

_____

_____

_____

_____

_____

_____

_____

6. Anonymity is a powerful spiritual principle.

Do a kind and generous deed for someone, and don't tell anyone. Humility is true spiritual power.

James 4:6 "God resists the proud, but gives <u>grace</u> to the humble.".

Your inspirational notes

_____

_____

_____

_____

_____

_____

_____

_____

_____

7. God's omnipotence.

No matter what I think or feel about any given situation or its circumstances; God truly is in charge; my responsibility is to accept it. My acceptance is what causes my spiritual growth.

Numbers 23:19 "<u>God is not a man</u>, that he should lie, nor a son of man, that he should repent. Has he said: and will he not do it? Or has he spoken and will he not make it good?"

Your inspirational notes

_____

_____

_____

_____

_____

_____

_____

_____

8. No man is an island.

I truly am not alone; I'm not the independent agent of my mind tells me that I am on this planet called Earth. Man is a social being needing the inter-action of others to maintain and sustain a healthy existence.

Hebrews 13:5 "<u>Let your conduct</u> be without covetousness and be content with such things as you have. For he himself has said "I will never leave you nor forsake you."

Your inspirational notes

_____

_____

_____

_____

_____

_____

_____

9. <u>Give</u> away what you <u>want</u> to keep.

This paradox seems almost foolish, until it is actually put into practice. You can't give away something you don't have. How can you expect to receive love by exhibiting hate; how can you share when you're selfish? How can you have a friend when you're not friendly?

Matthew 7:12 "Therefore, whatever you want men to do to you, do also to them, for this is the law all the prophets."

Your inspirational notes

_____

_____

_____

_____

_____

_____

_____

_____

10. Strive to be a better servant.

How can I sincerely best serve my fellow man? This question can be best answered by prayer and meditation; for each situation will differ.

Matthew 10:24-25 "A <u>disciple</u> is not above his <u>teacher</u>, nor a <u>servant</u> above his master. "It is enough for a disciple that he be like his teacher, and a servant like his master. If they have called the master of the house Beelzebub, how much more will they call those of his household?"

Your inspirational notes

_____

_____

_____

_____

_____

_____

_____

_____

11. Be a warrior of peace.

An interesting dichotomy is presented in this decla-
ration. There is a ongoing war unseen to the human
eye existing. Battle for that which is righteous and
noble and you will establish peace wherever you
stand; for where you stand shall be holy ground.

I Timothy 6:12 "Fight the good fight of
faith, lay hold on eternal life. To which
you were also called and have confessed
the good confession in the presence of
many witnesses."

Your inspirational notes

_____

_____

_____

_____

_____

_____

_____

12. Share more!!!

Even though I share my worldly belongings and possessions, there is so much more of me, that can be contributed back to the healthy flow of society.

Galatians 6:6 "Let him who is taught the share in all good things with him who teaches."

Your inspirational notes

_____

_____

_____

_____

_____

_____

_____

_____

_____

13. On being number two.

Being number one requires a tremendous amount of energy and effort on one's part. The top of the hill can present untold numbers of complications, such as unwanted fear, anxiety, over-precaution, irrational behavior, paranoia. Number two is a great position for learning.

Joshua 1:5 "No man shall be able to stand before all the days of your life, as I was with Moses so I will be with you. I will not leave or forsake you."

Your inspirational notes

_____

_____

_____

_____

_____

_____

_____

14. Be faithful.

Being faithful is a virtue of noble praise. Being faithful requires honesty, valor, trustworthiness, courage, perseverance, responsible and many more attributable characteristics.

Hebrews 11:6 "But without faith it is impossible to please Him; for he who comes to God must believe that He is and that H is a rewarder of those who diligently seek him."

Your inspirational notes

_____

_____

_____

_____

_____

_____

_____

_____

_____

15. Forgive and forget.

Forgiving is essential to healthy spiritual growth, for without it bitterness begins to take root in one's spirit. Forgetting is a more difficult task for some, due to the reoccurring emotional dilemma that these thoughts bring with them of reliving the event by memory.

Hebrews 12:15 "Looking diligently least anyone fall short of the grace of God; lest any root of bitterness springing up cause trouble, and by this many become defiled."

Your inspirational notes

_____

_____

_____

_____

_____

_____

_____

16. Submit to overcome and conquer.

By submitting we stop the principle of resistance.
The resistance is only as great as the force that is
applied against it. This simple principle can be
applied to a wide variety of circumstances. Just use
your imagination on this one, it seems unending.

> I Peter 2:13 "Therefore submit your-
> selves to every ordinance of man for the
> Lord's sake, whether to the King as
> supreme."

Your inspirational notes

_____

_____

_____

_____

_____

_____

_____

17. Men of faith are good examples to follow, while you sojourn here on Earth.

Most young children today will look up to whatever athlete is in the limelight or cleaver new upstart business enterprise becomes the next billionaire. All this is vanity; perishable trivia to be lost. Seek that which is eternal and non-perishable.

Hebrews 11:1-2 "Now faith is the substance of things hoped for, the evidence of things not seen, for by it the elders obtained a good testimony."

Your inspirational notes

_____

_____

_____

_____

_____

_____

_____

18. Don't live in the past; however let it not be forgotten; for it is the key to your future.

The old proverb of if you don't remember the past, your destined to relive it is true. What you fail to correct will continually reoccur if forgotten. The past is a reservoir of information to be drawn from when needed.

Philippians 3:13 "Brethren, I do not count myself to have apprehended but one thing I do forgetting those things which are behind and reaching forward to those things which are ahead."

Your inspirational notes

_____

_____

_____

_____

_____

_____

_____

19. Learn to love humility.

Humility is a virtue no one learns at the college or university of choice. It's the painstaking process of experiencing life on life terms and being subjugated to the realities of pain and suffering all must go through living and growing spiritually and developing grace fully toward Christ.

Proverbs 22:4 "By <u>humility</u> and the <u>fear</u> of the Lord are <u>riches</u> and <u>honor</u> and <u>life</u>."

Your inspirational notes

_____

_____

_____

_____

_____

_____

_____

_____

20. Serve others more!!!

Man's selfishness has caused him to create a world of competiveness and distortion beyond the norm of his intellectual capacity to correct the errors created. In the short of it; it's a world out of control, based on being number one.

Galatians 5:13 "For you, brethren, have been called to liberty; only do not use liberty as an opportunity for the flesh, but through love serve one another."

Your inspirational notes

_____

_____

_____

_____

_____

_____

_____

_____

21. Be a peacemaker.

There is so much confusion and chaos in the world; due to greed, selfishness, fear, lying and many more variables. Dare to be a peacemaker and like salmon, swim against the normal flow of current.

Matthew 5:9 "Blessed are the peace-makers for they shall be called <u>sons</u> of God."

Your inspirational notes

_____

_____

_____

_____

_____

_____

_____

_____

_____

22. Make wise decisions.

Most mature, responsible people who are honest with themselves will tell that their lives have been directed by the choices and decisions they have made.

II Timothy 3:14-15 "But as far as you, continue in the things which you have learned and been assured of knowing from whom you have learn them, and that from childhood you have known the holy scriptures which are able to make you wise for salvation through faith which is in Christ Jesus."

Your inspirational notes

_____

_____

_____

_____

_____

_____

_____

23. Accept my character defects.

By accepting my own character defects, I can first realize my true self. Looking honestly at myself, introspective observation gets better and better and growth becomes easier and easier. More importantly, accepting others gets more realistic, and I join in the human race as a participant as opposed to an outsider picking others apart.

Romans 12:3 "For I say, through the grace given to me, to everyone who is among you, not to think of himself more highly than he ought to <u>think</u>, but to think soberly as God has dealt to each one a <u>measure of faith</u>."

Your inspirational notes

_____

_____

_____

_____

_____

_____

_____

24. Accept others defects.

By accepting others defects, I'm assured that I've accepted my own. It is truly impossible to see something that you're not looking for or searching to find. We all find what we look for.

Ephesians 1:6 "To the praise of the glory of His grace, by which He has made us accepted in the Beloved."

Your inspirational notes

_____

_____

_____

_____

_____

_____

_____

_____

25. Look more at the bigger picture for your life.

We can only accomplish that which we are able to see. If we're only looking at a very little segment of an event that's all we can see and grow to, however by looking at the wide panoramic view we grow to see what we look for.

> Genesis 13:14 "And the Lord said to Abram after Lot had separated from Him: "lift your eyes now and look from the place where you are – northward, southward, eastward, and westward. For all the land which you see I give to you and your descendants forever."

Your inspirational notes

_____

_____

_____

_____

_____

_____

_____

26. Don't always seek to be right.

Being right constantly puts one in a position of authority or supremacy. Being always right eventually will lead one to the seat of being the judger of others.

Matthew 7:1-2 "Judge not that you be not judged. For with what judgment you judge, you will be judged, and with the spare measure you use it will measured back to you."

Your inspirational notes

_____

_____

_____

_____

_____

_____

_____

_____

_____

27. Encourage others.

By encouraging others you will strengthen yourself, also it's another way to get out of your own
selfishness.

I Corinthians 14:31 "For you can all
prophesy one by one, that all may learn
and all may be encouraged."

Your inspirational notes

_____

_____

_____

_____

_____

_____

_____

_____

_____

28. Crucify your flesh.

By denying your fleshly nature of its wants and desires you will be resisting your greatest enemy. Our worst enemy is not outside of us but our own desires and pleasures.

Galatians 2:20 "I have been crucified with Christ, it is no longer who live but Christ lives in me, and the life which I now live in the flesh I live by faith in the son of God who loves me and gave Himself for me."

Your inspirational notes

_____

_____

_____

_____

_____

_____

_____

_____

29. No favoritism.

There are no favorites with God; He deals with us all the same. Though it sometimes would appear that some are more blessed than others, it's all based on free will choices of spiritual principles we make.

Galatians 2:6 "But from those who seemed to be something – whatever they were, it make no difference to me; God shows personal favoritism to no man – for those who seemed to be something added nothing to me."

Your inspirational notes

_____

_____

_____

_____

_____

_____

_____

30. Show others who are ready to be shown.

There is nothing more unrewarding than trying your best to help someone who doesn't believe they need help, and you're fully aware that they do. Many are in need of your knowledge and experience, pray to find them and they will appear.

Galatians 6:2 "Bear one another's burden, and so fulfill the law of Christ."

Your inspirational notes

_____

_____

_____

_____

_____

_____

_____

31. Be more loving.

If; but just once a day; a person would do a kind loving act toward another human being the world could be drastically changed in a relatively short time.

Matthew 22:39 "You shall love your neighbor as yourself."

Your inspirational notes

_____

_____

_____

_____

_____

_____

_____

_____

_____

32. Be kinder to people.

Be genuinely kind to people and they will over a period of time wonder why you are so different from the rest of those around them.

Galatians 5:22 "But the fruit of the spirit is love, joy, peace, long-suffering, <u>kindness</u>, goodness, faithfulness, gentleness, self-control, against such there is no law."

Your inspirational notes

_____

_____

_____

_____

_____

_____

_____

_____

33. Read more spiritual literature.

True is the statement, faith comes by hearing the word of God. By reading the word your own mind nears the word as you meditate and contemplate on what you are reading.

I Timothy 4:13 "Till I come, give attention to reading, to exhortation, to doctrine."

Your inspirational notes

_____

_____

_____

_____

_____

_____

_____

_____

_____

34. Ask God more for help.

By seeking God's advice and guidance; over a period of time and that time period will be determined by you; one will feel the assurance of his power in making decisions, awkwardly at first, I'm sure, then more assuredly as time goes on.

Psalms 33:20 "Our soul waits for the Lord; He is our help and our shield."

Your inspirational notes

_____

_____

_____

_____

_____

_____

_____

_____

35. Give more of your time to others.

Time is a decreasing commodity that we all possess. By sharing more of our time with others, especially loved ones such as children, spouses, siblings, we can truly share our most precious asset.

Psalms 89:47 "Remember how short my time is, for what futility have you created all the children of men."

Your inspirational notes

_____

_____

_____

_____

_____

_____

_____

_____

36. Broaden your vision.

A person is only able to grow and develop as much as their mind will allow them to think. If you think small and little things that will be your growth pattern. If you think big and expansive so will your growth pattern be.

Psalms 118:5 "I called on the Lord in distress; the Lord answered me and set me in a broad place."

Your inspirational notes

_____

_____

_____

_____

_____

_____

_____

_____

37. Return good for evil.

Don't return evil for evil; for the evil will never
be destroyed. As the light dispels the darkness;
so does good dispel evil.

Romans 12:21 "Do not be overcome by
evil but overcome evil with good."

Your inspirational notes

_____

_____

_____

_____

_____

_____

_____

_____

_____

38. Look for the spiritual aspects of everyday life more than you are currently doing.

In our everyday lives the spiritual answers to questions we've prayed for or answers sought are occurring. We're just too busy living life to realize it. You will only see what you look for.

I Corinthians 2:15 "But he who is spiritual judges all things, yet he himself is rightly judged by no one."

Your inspirational notes

_____

_____

_____

_____

_____

_____

_____

_____

_____

39. Be empathic towards others.

Being empathic with others is a sure way to show the love of Christ in your life. Because of Christ compassionate, empathic love toward us we have opportunity for redemption and an example of true love to follow.

Romans 13:8 "Owe no one anything except to love one another, for he who loves another has fulfilled the law."

Your inspirational notes

_____

_____

_____

_____

_____

_____

_____

_____

40. Search even deeper into yourself to serve others.

There truly is no greater service to our fellow man to be of service to them.

Romans 12:1 "I beseech you therefore brethren, by the mercies of God, that you present your bodies a living sacrifice, holy, acceptable to God, which is your reasonable service."

Your inspirational notes

_____

_____

_____

_____

_____

_____

_____

_____

_____

41. Make others feel they are special.

All of us at times in this life feel lost or lonely and confused no matter how spiritual we are or think we are. We all need to feel wanted and special on occasion.

Psalms 30:5 "For His anger is but for a moment, His favor is for a life; weeping may endure for a night but joy comes in the morning."

Your inspirational notes

_____

_____

_____

_____

_____

_____

_____

_____

42. Am I self-searching?

Am I searching my inner self to look at areas in my life that can be improved on and further developed? We can all improve.

II Corinthians 10:18 "For not he who commends himself is approved, but whom the Lord commends."

Your inspirational notes

_____

_____

_____

_____

_____

_____

_____

_____

43. Pray for a more spiritual perception.

God will give us what we ask Him for. If we don't ask for those spiritual attributes that are beneficial for not only ourselves as well as those around us. How do we expect to receive them?

I John 5:14 "Now this is the confidence that we have in Him, that if we ask anything according to His will, He hears us."

Your inspirational notes

_____

_____

_____

_____

_____

_____

_____

_____

44. Be tolerable of others.

Being tolerable of others will give one a true sense of humility. By understanding tolerance of others, give one a true perspective of themselves to others.

Romans 12:3 "For I say, through the grace given to me, to everyone who is among you, not to think of himself more highly than he ought to think, but to think soberly, as God has dealt to each one a measure of faith."

Your inspirational notes

_____

_____

_____

_____

_____

_____

_____

45. Think noble thoughts.

The thought that we think determine our actions, which in turn our character and ultimately our destination in life. No one chooses his or her place of birth, however we determine our destination.

Philippians 4:8 "Finally, brethren, whatever things are true, whatever things are noble, whatever things are just, whatever things are pure, whatever things are lovely, whatever things are of good report, it there is any virtue and if there is anything praiseworthy meditate on these things."

Your inspirational notes

_____

_____

_____

_____

_____

_____

46. Show no partiality.

Showing no partiality can truly be Christ-like in application. Christ showed no preference in His time on Earth and when performing His miracles. His long standing, everlasting command of love they neighbor as thyself still stands and epitomizes non-partiality.

James 2:9 "But if you show partiality you commit sin, and are convicted by the law as transgressors."

Your inspirational notes

_____

_____

_____

_____

_____

_____

_____

47. Be rational.

Be rational in your thinking, you will eventually come to a place of serenity and peace in your spirit, mind, and soul.

Philippians 2:5-6 "Let this mind be in you which was also in Christ Jesus who being in the form of God, did not consider it robbery to be equal with God."

Your inspirational notes

_____

_____

_____

_____

_____

_____

_____

_____

48. Persevere.

You must continue on in the royal and noble call which you've undertaken, for truly your work for and with the Lord is rewarded.

II John 8 "Look to yourselves that we do not lose those things we worked for, but that we may receive a full reward."

Your inspirational notes

_____

_____

_____

_____

_____

_____

_____

_____

49. Live free of bondage.

Bondage of any type whether it be emotional, physical, spiritual, or another form separates us from the true blessings of God.

Romans 8:14-15 "For as many as are led by the spirit of God, these are sons of God. For you did not receive the spirit of bondage again to fear but you received the spirit of adoption by whom we cry out Abba Father."

Your inspirational notes

_____

_____

_____

_____

_____

_____

_____

_____

50. Forgive others.

Forgiving others on occasion can be a painful unrelenting process. Those we know who have purposely harmed us can make this very difficult, none the less we must do it.

Matthew 6:14-15 "For if you forgive men their trespasses, your heavenly Father will also forgive you. But if you do not forgive men their trespasses, neither will your Father forgive your trespasses."

Your inspirational notes

_____

_____

_____

_____

_____

_____

_____

51. No matter whom falls persevere and go forward.

Each one of us will stand before God and be judged. My wife or my children or parents or friends are going to speak on my behalf on judgment day.

Romans 14:12 "So then each of us shall give account of himself to God."

Your inspirational notes

_____

_____

_____

_____

_____

_____

_____

_____

_____

52. Be of service to those around you.

Being of service to those around you can be exciting and spiritually satisfying. In service is one way to fulfill the law of humility.

James 4:6 "God resists the proud but gives grace to the humble."

Your inspirational notes

_____

_____

_____

_____

_____

_____

_____

_____

_____

53. Share joy.

The joy of the Lord is our strength. How better
to help those around us than to share with them
this wondrous gift from the Lord.

Psalms 16:11 "You will show me the path
of life; in your presence is fullness of joy
at your right hand are pleasures forever-
more."

Your inspirational notes

—

_____

_____

_____

_____

_____

_____

_____

_____

54. Give more of your time to others.

Giving more of your time to others will not only give you an opportunity to share yourself, but also to learn from the others that you share with.

Galatians 6:6 "Let him who is taught the word share in all good things with him who teaches."

Your inspirational notes

_____

_____

_____

_____

_____

_____

_____

_____

55. Be understanding of those around you.

When a person is gifted or talented being around "normal" people can be a taxing dilemma on occasion. Spiritually speaking, God has blessed us all with different abilities.

Proverbs 4:7 "Wisdom is the principle thing therefore get wisdom and in all your getting get understanding."

Your inspirational notes

_____

_____

_____

_____

_____

_____

_____

_____

56. Seek peace and to be a peacemaker.

Peacemakers have a special place in our world. First you have to make peace with yourself before you can make peace with anyone else.

Matthew 5:9 "Blessed are the peacemakers, for they shall be called sons of God."

Your inspirational notes

_____

_____

_____

_____

_____

_____

_____

_____

_____

57. Work on yourself.

One can only definitively work on themselves. The best way that I've come to believe to help others is to be good example to those around you. As opposed to do as I say, do as I do seems to be a better choice.

Romans 6:7 and 6:18 "For he who has died has been freed from sin. And having been set free from sin, you became slaves of righteousness."

Your inspirational notes

_____

_____

_____

_____

_____

_____

_____

_____

58. Forgiveness.

This topic is again addressed because of its importance to a healthy spiritual life. Unforgiveness can be the door that keeps us locked in the cesspool of bitterness, and by this many have become defiled. Those who are defiled have defiled themselves by their unforgiveness.

> Hebrews 12:15 "Looking diligently lest anyone fall short of the grace of God; lest any root of bitterness springing up cause trouble and by this many become defiled."

Your inspirational notes

_____

_____

_____

_____

_____

_____

_____

59. Patience.

Contrary to what you may have heard, patience is not a negative position in life. Patience requires faith, strength, endurance, wisdom, and self-suffering and sacrifice.

Hebrews 6:12 "That you do not become sluggish but imitate those who through faith and patience inherit the promises."

Your inspirational notes

_____

_____

_____

_____

_____

_____

_____

_____

60. Strive for emotional balance.

To strive is to contend or struggle against someone or something. To stay on a emotional
balance is a daily effort which gives us a better
perspective on our own life's ups and downs;
but more importantly others when this occurs
we are in a much better position to help others
because we are emotionally stable.

Job 3:16 "Let me be weighed in a just balance, that God may know my integrity."

Your inspirational notes

_____

_____

_____

_____

_____

_____

_____

_____

61. Do what you do out of love.

If what you do is not out of love, your motive is not honest. It's as if you pose the statement, "Let your yes be yes and your no be no for more than this is from the wicked one.

Levi 19:18 "You shall not take vengeance, nor bear any grudge against the children of your people, but you shall love your neighbor as yourself; I am the Lord."

Your inspirational notes

_____

_____

_____

_____

_____

_____

_____

_____

62. Truth and peace are essential wherever you go.

Life is such a plethora of circumstances and events, that if you can as you go through your normal day's activities as best you can establish truth and peace. By doing this not only will you grow spiritually but those around you will benefit.

John 8:32 "And you shall know the truth and the truth shall make you free."

Your inspirational notes

_____

_____

_____

_____

_____

_____

_____

_____

63. Practice love and tolerance.

By practicing both of these together not only will you develop patience but a better understanding of what it means to understand than to be understood.

Psalms 119:165 "Great peace have those who love your law, and nothing causes them to stumble."

Your inspirational notes

_____

_____

_____

_____

_____

_____

_____

_____

_____

64. Hope brings spiritual growth.

Hope brings spiritual growth, by putting you in a positive mental attitude of looking forward in any given situation. By hoping you're practicing faith, patience, love, and there is no defense against these spiritual principles.

Romans 5:5 "Now hope does not disappoint because the love of God has been poured out in our hearts by the Holy Spirit who was given to us."

Your inspirational notes

_____

_____

_____

_____

_____

_____

_____

65. Emotional pain is my choice to choose.

In life very often, we are not the victim of events around us, but choose how they effect us. The same event can happen to two people and have two different outcomes based on their emotional choice in the matter.

Galatians 6:7 "Do not be deceived, God is not mocked; for whatever a man sows, that he will also reap."

Your inspirational notes

_____

_____

_____

_____

_____

_____

_____

_____

66. Principles are permanent.

Principles once they have been established are unchanging. When spiritual principles are applied to a life they will yield their intended results every time. My said your responsibility is be consistent in their use.

Hebrews 5:12 "For though by this time you ought to be teachers you need some-one to teach you again the first principles of the oracles of God; and you have come to need milk and not sold food."

Your inspirational notes

_____

_____

_____

_____

_____

_____

_____

67. Righteousness is my goal.

My goal on a daily basis must be to be as right-eous as I possibly can. Living a righteous life is a process we must undertake on a daily basis. By doing this on a daily basis it's not over-whelming and becomes extremely doable to us as an accomplishment.

Psalms 19:2 "Day unto day utters speech, and night unto night reveals knowledge."

Your inspirational notes

_____

_____

_____

_____

_____

_____

_____

_____

68. Recovery and restoration.

Recovery and restoration go hand in hand together. Having fallen from grace in the garden of Eden, all men must go through the process of recovering our true position in the universe as children of God. Restoration occurs when this happens as men and women of God.

Acts 3:21 "Whom Heaven must receive until the times of restoration of all things, which God has spoken by the mouth of all holy prophets since the world began."

Your inspirational notes

_____

_____

_____

_____

_____

_____

_____

69. Don't expect too much from others; do it yourself.

Life is a rather simple event when we do our best at whatever task is in front of us to do. Learn to rely more on yourself and God than others and your satisfaction and self approval will be long-lasting.

Joel 2:13 "So rend your heart and not your garments, return to the Lord your God, for he is gracious and merciful, slow to anger and of great kindness and he relents from doing harm."

Your inspirational notes

_____

_____

_____

_____

_____

_____

_____

70. Service to others is a great way to be rid of self-ishness.

By serving others, we aren't involved in our own lives, getting out of ourselves is also a say of developing spiritual growth in altruistic behavior as Jesus was doing.

Romans 12:1 "I beseech you therefore brethren, by the mercies of God, that you present your bodies a living sacrifice, holy acceptable to God, which is your reasonable service."

Your inspirational notes

_____

_____

_____

_____

_____

_____

_____

71. Don't hold back your affection from those you love.

The life we live here on Earth is so short and temporary in the comparison of time, that those we love ought to be our priority.

James 4:14 "Whereas you do not know what will happen tomorrow. For what is your life? It is even a vapor that appears for a little time and then vanishes away."

Your inspirational notes

_____

_____

_____

_____

_____

_____

_____

_____

_____

_____

72. Pursue perfection.

Perfection is a word in the Hebrew language which means maturity. So therefore it truly can be attained. Perfection in all areas of your life.

Hebrews 6:1 "Therefore, leaving the discussion of the elementary principles of Christ, let us go on to perfection, not laying again the foundation of repentance from dead works and of faith toward God."

Your inspirational notes

_____

_____

_____

_____

_____

_____

_____

73. Never give up hope that your situation will improve.

Hope is a spiritual principle, which will always bring you forward and through any obstacle with a renewed sense of vigor and strength.

Psalms 39:7 "And now, Lord, what do I want for? My hope is in you."

Your inspirational notes

_____

_____

_____

_____

_____

_____

_____

_____

_____

74. Forgiveness is the pathway to self-healing.

Self-healing starts by our ability to forgive ourselves from past offenses others have done to us. Offenses we have done to others relieve us of our guilt. The healing process starts when we start it by our forgiveness.

Psalms 103:3-4 "If you Lord, should mark iniquities, O Lord, who could stand? But there is forgiveness with you."

Your inspirational notes

_____

_____

_____

_____

_____

_____

_____

_____

75. Love conquers all obstacles.

Love is the overwhelming force that regardless of the obstacle will overcome. There is nothing greater in the spiritual world or the natural than love.

I Corinthians 13:13 "And now abide faith, hope, love these three, but the greatest of these is love."

Your inspirational notes

_____

_____

_____

_____

_____

_____

_____

_____

_____

76. Principles.

When we live by principles, we put ourselves on a higher plane of existence and thought. The statement that energy seeks its own level is a truism, whether it be spiritual, physical or mental it's our choice.

Philippians 4:8 "Finally, brethren, whatever things are true, whatever things are noble, whatever things are just, whatever things are lovely, whatever things are of good report, if there is any virtue and if there is anything praiseworthy meditate on these things."

Your inspirational notes

_____

_____

_____

_____

_____

_____

_____

79. Give your best.

Giving your best is a test that only you and God can truly know. If you have done so it will self motivate you to do better at whatever it is you attempt on a consistent basis.

> John 3:16 "For God so loved the world that He gave His only begotten Son, that whosoever believes in Him should not perish but have everlasting life."

Your inspirational notes

_____

_____

_____

_____

_____

_____

_____

_____

80. Create a larger view of your own vision.

We can only go as far as we can see. The goal you set is the goal you will accomplish.

> Genesis 13:14-15 "And the Lord said to Abram after Lot had separated from Him: "Lift your eyes now and look from the place where you are northward, southward, eastward, and westward for all the land which you see I give to you and your descendants forever."

Your inspirational notes

_____

_____

_____

_____

_____

_____

_____

_____

81. As much as you can in your power, make peace with those around you.

Peace like love is an action, I must do something in a positive way to activate the process.

Romans 12:18-19 "If it is possible, as much as depends on you, live peaceably with all men. Beloved, do not avenge yourselves, but rather give lace to wrath; for it is written, vengeance is mine I will repay," says the Lord."

Your inspirational notes

_____

_____

_____

_____

_____

_____

_____

_____

82. Be righteous.

Being righteous simply means doing the right thing or action at the appropriate time. The right thing pertaining to the word of God.

Psalms 146:8 "The Lord opens the eyes of the blind; the Lord raises those who are bowed down; the Lord loves the righteous."

Your inspirational notes

_____

_____

_____

_____

_____

_____

_____

_____

_____

83. Expand your faith.

We are truly only limited by our ability to imagine. As our faith grows and we move higher in our spiritual understanding, we become aware that it was our own thinking that stifle our growth.

Luke 2:52 "And Jesus increased in wisdom and stature and in favor with God and men."

Your inspirational notes

_____

_____

_____

_____

_____

_____

_____

_____

84. Practice as best you can to react spiritually mature to events going on around you in everyday life.

Practice is the most important word in the above aforementioned sentence. By practicing indicates that we're not going to get it correct the first time; maybe not even the first ten times. There has to be a starting point, so we commence our journey to achieve our goal, spiritual maturity. By the way this is a lifelong endeavor.

Hebrews 6:1 "Therefore, leaving the discussion of the elementary . principles of Christ, let us go on to perfection, not laying again the foundation of repentance form dead works and of faith toward God."

Your inspirational notes

_____

_____

_____

_____

_____

_____

_____

85. Work to show yourself approved to God and others will want your help.

No one gets to Heaven by works; however works are our outward manifestation of our inner spiritual condition. Since my journey here on Earth is shared event, others will notice my behavior and question why I do what I do. When this occurs and it will, it's my opportunity to explain by belief in Jesus Christ.

II Timothy 2:15 "Be diligent to present yourself approved to God, a worker who does not need to be ashamed, rightly dividing the word of truth."

Your inspirational notes

_____

_____

_____

_____

_____

_____

_____

86. Always strive for perfection.

As was previously written on Droplet #72, perfection is to be spiritually mature. What I must do in order to be aware of my own growth is strive for this spiritually state of perfection in all my affairs. The act that this thought actually comes in my conscious is a sign of spiritual growth on my part.

Psalms 119:96 "I have seen the consummation of all perfection, but your commandment is exceedingly broad."

Your inspirational notes

_____

_____

_____

_____

_____

_____

_____

_____

87. Persevere in the ways of Jesus Christ, no matter what the circumstances are.

Most Christians are willing to follow Christ, while the miracle of the wedding feast of wine is being drank. When the cup of gall is being presented, at the cross, there are not many to be found.

> Proverbs 9:62 "But Jesus said to him, 'No one, having pot in his hand to the plow, and looking back is fit for the kingdom of God.'"

Your inspirational notes

_____

_____

_____

_____

_____

_____

_____

_____

88. Keep your spiritual channel open, by allowing the flow of ideas.

Just as the mountain stream is fresh and clear, our minds operate in a similar way. When a free flow of water is stopped up, over a period of time it becomes stagnant and foul smelling. What's backing up the spiritual flow of your own mind? Bitterness, unforiveness, hatred, resentment, fear, anger, lying...

John 4:14 "Whoever drinks of the water that I shall give him will never thirst. But the water that I shall give him will become in him a foundation of water springing up into everlasting life."

Your inspirational notes

_____

_____

_____

_____

_____

_____

89. Learn as much as you can about men and women of God.

One of the greatest revelations I've received from God, has been that I can experience other's triumphs and defeats, by reading about their lives. By myself I have only one life of experiences, by doing the above mentioned paragraph, I can have multiple.

Romans 15:4 "For whatever things were written before were written for our learning that we through the patience and comfort of the scriptures might have hope."

Your inspirational notes

_____

_____

_____

_____

_____

_____

_____

90. Give preference to others.

Stop desiring to be number one, your ego won't miss it all. Seek to serve than to be catered to.

Matthew 20:16 "So the last will be first, and the first last. For many are called but few chosen."

Your inspirational notes

_____

_____

_____

_____

_____

_____

_____

_____

_____

91. Excel in righteousness.

There is not a position to high to attain in this area
of our spiritual growth. You will never get to the
top so to speak or be number one at the righteous.
The journey is the peak of highest expectation.

Galatians 5:22-23 "But the fruit of the spirit
is love, joy, peace, long suffering, kindness,
goodness, faithfulness, gentleness, self-control against such there is no law."

Your inspirational notes

_____

_____

_____

_____

_____

_____

_____

_____

92. Use your time here on Earth for the service of God.

Truly time is such an elusive entity and none can hold it back. Time marches forward against all expectations, while everyone looks back at what could have been. Everyone gets allotted a certain amount of time, and no one knows that allotment.

James 4:14 "Whereas you do not know what will happen tomorrow, for what is your life? It is even a vapor, that appears for a little time and then vanishes away."

Your inspirational notes

_____

_____

_____

_____

_____

_____

_____

_____

93. Simplicity.

The adage keep it simple stupid has validity.
The human mind is so complex; science after all
these years of research, still hasn't figured it out,
yet. The statement God is love is simplicity at its
best and most people still don't get it.

II Corinthians 1:12 "For our boasting is
this: testimony of our conscience. That
we conducted ourselves in the world in
simplicity and godly sincerity, not with
flashy wisdom but by the grace of God,
and more abundantly toward you."

Your inspirational notes

_____

_____

_____

_____

_____

_____

94. Humility.

Humility does not mean that you are a doormat or someone's whipping post, nor does it mean that you're a subservient human to those around you. True humility consists of dignity, honor, respect and self esteem.

I Peter 5:5 "Likewise you younger people submit yourselves to your elders. Yes all of you be submissive to one another and be cloaked with humility for "God resists the proud, but gives grace to the humble."

Your inspirational notes

_____

_____

_____

_____

_____

_____

95. Patience through trials.

Patience through trials is not an easy task to perform. Most of us during some trials or spiritual tests we are undergoing, want it over as soon as possible. However, by patience and endurance we develop our character and God's trust to handle even more.

James 1:2-3 "My brethren count it all joy when you fall into various trials, knowing that the testing of your faith produces patience."

Your inspirational notes

_____

_____

_____

_____

_____

_____

_____

96. Wait on the Lord.

Allow God to do things in His timing and not your own. There is a divine time for events that God has ordained, before time began in our finite minds. My responsibility and yours is to learn to wait on God.

Isaiah 40:31 "But those who wait on the Lord, shall renew their strength, they shall mount up with wings like eagles, they shall run and not grow weary, they shall walk and not faint."

Your inspirational notes

_____

_____

_____

_____

_____

_____

_____

97. Walk as much as you can as the Lord walked.

This may sound like a tall order, however Paul who was a sinner just like you and me did it.

I Corinthians 11:1 "Imitate me, just as I also imitate Christ."

Your inspirational notes

_____

_____

_____

_____

_____

_____

_____

_____

_____

98. Be faithful in what God ask you to do.

Whatever God ask you to do is an opportunity to show your faithfulness and obedience. Regardless of how insignificant we find the request, do it to the best of your ability.

Luke 16:10 "He who is faithful in what is least is faithful also in much and he who is unjust in what is least is unjust also in much."

Your inspirational notes

_____

_____

_____

_____

_____

_____

_____

_____

_____

99. Be diligent.

Diligence regardless of circumstances will propel you forward in the direction of righteousness, if you slip and get off the right way.

Revelation 3:10 "Because you have kept my command to persevere I also will keep you from the hour of trial which shall come upon the whole world, to test those who dwell on the Earth."

Your inspirational notes

_____

_____

_____

_____

_____

_____

_____

_____

100. Continue in humility and you will always be aware of these principles mentioned in this book.

Humility is truly the spiritual key that opens the door to God's holy tool box, which has all the spiritual help you need to survive in this world we live in.

I Peter 5:6 "Therefore humble yourselves under the mighty hand of God that He may exalt you in due time."

Your inspirational notes

_____

_____

_____

_____

_____

_____

_____

_____

Conclusion:

Is there really a conclusion? Once having accepted Christ we have eternal life in Him. However in this stage of our existence, here on earth we do all those human things we can as a spiritual being trapped in our bodies. Truly experiences, pain, suffering, joy, happiness, sadness, and so many other human emotions.

Acceptance is my first step toward growth of spiritual knowledge of myself. I can only work on me and by doing so the others around me change. Use the lessons wisely and God will show you what you need to work on in your own personal life.

Love is the fulfillment of the Law; in so doing all the Law and commandments are in subject to love.

If you know to do these things, then do them and be blessed with all the spiritual blessings in Christ.

Thank you for helping my ministry with Jesus Christ.

God bless you.